HOW CAN I *FEEL* Closer to GOD?

CHRIS MORPHEW

Illustrated by Emma Randall

thegoodbook
COMPANY

To Josiah and Mim

How Can I Feel Closer to God?
© Chris Morphew 2023.

Published by:
The Good Book Company

thegoodbook.com | thegoodbook.co.uk
thegoodbook.com.au | thegoodbook.co.nz | thegoodbook.co.in

ISBN: 9781784988357 | Printed in the UK

Illustrated by Emma Randall | Design by André Parker

"*Who Am I and Why Do I Matter?* takes one of the core truths of Scripture and explains it in a way that middle-schoolers (and their parents) can understand. I can't wait to put this into my children's hands, and also encourage them to put it into the hands of their unbelieving friends."

JOHN PERRITT, Director of Resources, Reformed Youth Ministries; Author, *Insecure: Fighting Our Lesser Fears with a Greater One*; Host, Local Youth Worker Podcast; father of five

"Chris is the teacher you wish you had. He gets where you're coming from and takes your questions—and you—seriously."

DR NATASHA MOORE, Research Fellow, Centre for Public Christianity

"What an excellent series—seriously excellent! I am certain Chris Morphew's chatty style, clear explanations, relevant illustrations and personal insights will engage, inform and equip tweens as they work through some of the big questions they and their peers will be asking."

TAMAR POLLARD, Families Minister, Wahroonga Anglican Church, Sydney, Australia

"Reading a Chris Morphew book is like sitting with a friend, with an open Bible between you, asking all the tough questions that are on your heart and getting solid, straight, honest answers that line up with God's word—answers that bring you to the light and hope and truth of Jesus. I love friends like that!"

COLIN BUCHANAN, Singer/Songwriter

Contents

Chapter 1

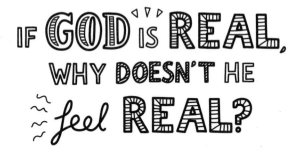

IF GOD IS REAL, WHY DOESN'T HE feel REAL?

The bell had just gone and the rest of my Christian Studies class were busy packing up their things, when one of my students—maybe 7 years old—found me at the front of the room and said, "Mr Morphew, I have a problem."

"What's up?" I asked, crouching to her eye level.

"The thing is," she said, "I know Jesus is real in *here*—" She tapped the side of her head. Then she lowered her hand and patted it against her chest. "—but I still don't know if he's real in *here*."

This kid had been learning about Jesus here at school for years now. She was smart and thoughtful, and she had plenty of information. But now she was discovering something that millions of others before her have learned about God:

Believing he loves you is one thing.

Actually *feeling* that love is something else.

The Bible makes some huge promises about the friendship God offers us as we put our trust in Jesus.

Jesus says he's come to lead us into the best life possible— life to the full (John 10 v 10).

He says if we're exhausted and stressed, we just need to come to him and he'll give us rest and peace, even in the middle of all life's chaos (Matthew 11 v 28; John 14 v 27; Philippians 4 v 6-7).

If we need wisdom for any situation, the Bible says to just trust God and ask, and he'll give it to us (James 1 v 5).

We're told that Jesus came to bring his friends a total life transformation—a change as huge and powerful as a caterpillar's transformation into a butterfly (Romans 8 v 29; Galatians 4 v 19). The Bible says that as we put our trust in Jesus, his Spirit comes to live in us, filling us with more and more of his love, joy, peace, patience, kindness, goodness, faithfulness, gentleness and self-control (Galatians 5 v 22-23).

Which sounds really great and everything.

But is it *true*?

I mean, is that what you're experiencing in your life right now? Complete, caterpillar-to-butterfly-level transformation? Or does this all seem like a bunch of nice ideas that don't actually work out in real life?

You pray, but nothing seems to happen.

You open the Bible, but it all just seems confusing and irrelevant.

You go to church and struggle to stay awake.

Meanwhile, you look around at your friends who don't follow Jesus, and they seem to be getting on just fine without him.

Does it feel like you're missing something? Like you've failed, somehow? Or like God's failed you?

All those promises might *sound* great—but if they don't work out in real life, then what's the point?

If God is real, why doesn't he *feel* real?

If God wants to be close to us, why does he often feel so far away?

Imagine a new kid shows up at your school. You see them across the room and think to yourself, *Maybe I'll be friends with that person.*

But not yet, obviously. I mean, you don't want to rush into things. First you need to figure out what their deal is. So you don't talk to them yet. You just watch from a distance.

You see them lean over to talk to someone, but they're too far away for you to hear. You sidle up behind them, trying to listen in—but unfortunately, the teacher sees you out of your seat and sends you back to your work.

At lunch, you spot the new kid sitting down to eat with some other people from your year. They invite you to join them, but you wave them off. After all, you're still completing your investigation. You wait until their backs are turned and sneak into the bushes behind them. You raise your binoculars, focus them in on the new kid, and pull out a notebook to record your observations: hair colour, eye colour, height, food preferences, chewing technique...

It's amazing what you can learn when you study someone closely enough.

Later, you have class with the new kid again. They answer a question from the teacher—and it's a pretty good answer, actually. Almost too good, though, you know? Like, who are they trying to impress? You flip your notebook to a new page, write the words, KNOWS TOO MUCH, and underline them.

By the end of the day, your notebook is filling up, but you still feel like you've barely scratched the surface—and so when you get home, you do the obvious:

Stalk them online.

You find their socials, but unfortunately they're set to

private. Which is suspicious, right? I mean, what does this kid have to hide?

At school the next day, you point this out to a friend. They shoot you a weird look and say, "Well, why don't you just add them and see if they accept?"

You roll your eyes. "Yeah, right! What if they're some kind of weirdo?"

Fast-forward another few weeks. You've got heaps of great notes on the new kid. All those hours you've spent staking out their locker have really paid off! And yet somehow…

You can't quite figure it out. But for some reason, you don't feel like you actually *know* them any better than you did on their first day.

What's wrong with this picture?

Well, a bunch of things, obviously. But my point is to highlight the fact that knowing *about* someone and actually *knowing* someone are two very different things.

Hiding in the bushes with your binoculars might get you all kinds of *information* about a person, but it's unlikely to lead to any kind of actual *relationship*—because there's a massive difference between being someone's friend and being their stalker.

And the reason I bring this up is that I think it's all too

easy for us to end up treating God this way without even realising we're doing it. It's possible to spend all kinds of time and energy learning *about* God without ever reaching the point where we feel like we *know* him.

Of course, getting the facts about God straight in our heads is incredibly important. (And if you're interested, there's another book in this series called *How Do We Know That Christianity is Really True?* which outlines the solid historical evidence that Jesus really is who the Bible says he is.)

But that's only part of the picture.

Like with anyone else, the way to really get to know Jesus isn't by hanging back at a distance, just learning *about* him. It's by stepping into a friendship.

There's this story that my mum tells about how all this finally started making sense for her.

Mum had grown up learning about Jesus; she had a head full of facts about him. But there was still something holding her back. Could she *really* trust that it was all true? Could she really give her whole life to it?

When she asked her mum—my grandmother—about it, Grannie gave her what turned out to be some really excellent advice: "Why don't you just live as if it's true for a while and see what happens?"

In other words, why not run an experiment?

Rather than just learning *about* the promises of Jesus, try spending some time living as if those promises are true.

Rather than just gathering more information *about* Jesus, try spending some time building a friendship *with* Jesus.

And so that's just what my mum did.

She ran the experiment—and she's never looked back.

Because the more she lived as if Jesus' promises were true, the more she discovered that they actually *are*. The more she chased after a relationship *with* Jesus, rather than just gathering more information *about* Jesus, the more she experienced the truth of Jesus' love, not just as an idea, but as a living, breathing reality in her life.

Years later, my mum passed this same advice down to me—and years after that, I passed it on to that little girl in my class who was trying to move her knowledge about Jesus from her head to her heart. It's made all the difference in my life, and I'm convinced it can do the same for you.

Ok. But how do we actually *do* it?

How do we live as if the promises of Jesus are true?

How do we put down the binoculars, climb out of the bushes, and start building an actual friendship with Jesus?

Well, that's what the rest of this book is all about.

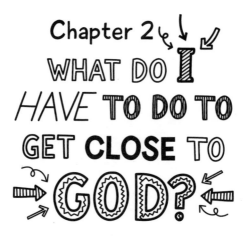

Chapter 2
WHAT DO I HAVE TO DO TO GET CLOSE TO GOD?

I want this book to be really practical.

As we go along, I'll suggest all kinds of things you can *do* to get to know God better, and to feel more closely connected to him. I hope these suggestions are really helpful—even life-changing!—but before we get into any of that, we need to be absolutely clear on something:

None of this is how we *become* friends with God.

The suggestions in this book aren't steps you need to take to get God to like you. This is not for one second about earning God's love or acceptance or approval.

Because friendship with God isn't a reward to be earned.

It's a gift to be received.

When you open the Bible, one of the first things you

discover is that friendship with God isn't meant to be just some nice little add-on to your life. It's what human beings were *created* for.

God made people to live in perfect friendship with him and with each other; he created us for lives of never-ending joy and peace and freedom, ruling and caring for God's good world, with God as our loving King (Genesis 1 v 26-28; 2 v 9).

Which sounds, a) fantastic, and, b) almost nothing like our lives today.

I mean, sure, we still experience passing moments of joy and peace and freedom—but we *also* experience sickness, suffering, injustice and death. And in the middle of all that, God often feels distant and hard to reach.

But according to the Bible, that's not because God has bailed on the friendship.

It's because we have.

See, another thing the Bible tells us about our friendship with God is that we've all made an absolute mess of it.

Instead of loving God and each other like we should, we sideline God and try to live however seems best to *us*. We see the evidence of this in big, obvious evil like war and murder—but also in a thousand everyday examples, like when we pretend not to notice someone who needs our help or cover up the truth to avoid getting into trouble.

In big ways and small, we all reject God's loving rule—and in the process, we bring chaos and destruction down on our world, on each other, and on our own hearts and souls.

And now that we've bailed on the friendship with God, we can't just tidy ourselves up and pretend everything's ok. The damage has been done. The relationship is broken, and no one could blame God for letting it stay that way. One way or another, whatever happens next is in his hands. If things are ever going to be made right again, we need *God* to make them right.

We need him to forgive us—to rescue us.

Thankfully, this is exactly what the good news of Jesus is all about.

In Jesus, God himself has come to our rescue.

During his time on Earth, Jesus showed what it looks like for a human being to live in perfect friendship with God, and with other people. He lived the perfect life of love that the rest of us have failed to live.

And then Jesus gave that life up for us.

Through his death, Jesus experienced all the consequences *we* deserve for turning our backs on God. Instead of bailing on us like we bailed on him, Jesus died to offer us forgiveness—to make a way for us to be welcomed back into the friendship—not as a reward to be earned, but as a free gift from God, paid for by Jesus' sacrifice on the cross.

The Bible puts it this way:

> *God saved you by his grace when you believed. And you can't take credit for this; it is a gift from God. Salvation is not a reward for the good things we have done, so none of us can boast about it. (Ephesians 2 v 8-9, NLT)*

We don't need to do one single thing to *earn* God's love and acceptance, because Jesus has already done everything it takes to welcome us home into friendship with God. All that's left for us to do is turn back to God and believe the good news (Mark 1 v 15).

But the story doesn't end there, because Jesus didn't stay dead. He came back to life, and he's still alive today, ruling the universe from heaven and preparing for the day he'll return to make this world our perfect home again.

On that day, God and his people will be perfectly united in the endless friendship we were created for and God will never feel distant or hard to reach again (Revelation 21 v 1-5)—which is amazing news!

But what's just as true, and just as amazing, is we don't have to wait until then.

Sure, our experience of God is going to get so much clearer and fuller when Jesus returns. But in the meantime, Jesus invites us into deep, life-changing friendship with him, right here, right now, *today*.

If you've spent much time reading the Bible, you might know that Jesus had a group of disciples who followed him around during his time on Earth—and that, right before he returned to heaven, he told *those* disciples to go out into all the world and make *more* disciples (Matthew 28 v 19-20).

Being a *disciple* is one of the main ways Jesus described the relationship he wants us to have with him (Matthew 16 v 24)—but outside the Bible, it's not a word we use very often.

So what does it *mean*, exactly?

Well, some people describe being a disciple as being a *follower* of Jesus—which isn't such a bad description. After all, Jesus *did* invite his first disciples to come and follow him (Matthew 4 v 19). But I'm not sure that gets us very far, because how on earth are we supposed to "follow" someone who is currently hanging out in another dimension, beyond our physical universe?

Meanwhile, for most of us, the place we most often talk about *following* people is on social media. And while I follow a bunch of celebrities online, it's not exactly a life-changing experience. (Plus, I'm pretty sure they don't even realise I'm doing it.)

Other people say being Jesus' disciple is like being his *student*—which I think is getting closer to what Jesus meant. But I'm guessing the idea that "following Jesus = more school" doesn't necessarily fill you with excitement. Besides, for most of us, the word *student* probably still makes us think of learning *about* Jesus, rather than actually getting to *know* Jesus.

Thankfully, I think there's a better way to understand this idea.

The writer Dallas Willard suggests that when we hear the word *disciple*, we should think *apprentice*—not a student falling asleep in the back of a classroom, but someone who's found the thing they most want to do in life, and who's getting on-the-job-training to learn how to do it.

Think of it this way: who's the person in the whole world you most deeply admire—the person who makes you say, "I wish I had their life! I wish I could learn to be like them, to do what they do!"?

Now, imagine that person actually calling you up and offering to help make it happen.

Imagine the Olympic gold medallist offering to be your personal coach so that *you* can go and compete in the Olympics.

Imagine the world-famous singer or actor or musician offering you private lessons so that *you* can learn to sing or act or play like them.

This is apprenticeship.

This is what Jesus wants to do for you—not just for your career, but for your *whole life*.

Jesus doesn't just want to save you *out* of the mess you've made of your friendship with God; he wants to save you *into* a whole new way of life, where you learn to trust that his way really is the best way to live, and get better and better at living it out (Matthew 7 v 24-27; John 13 v 17).

Again, this isn't how we *earn* our friendship with God.

The question isn't, "How much do you have to do to get God to love and accept you?" It's, "How much space do you want to open up in your life to *experience* God's love first-hand?"

As you put your trust in Jesus, he wants to lead you and guide you into the best life possible.

And the more you reshape your life around Jesus' life and teachings, the more you'll experience his love and joy and peace and freedom, not just as nice *ideas*, but as your actual day-to-day experience (John 10 v 10; John 15 v 5; Matthew 11 v 28-30).

Which all sounds great in theory.

So why doesn't it always feel that way in real life?

Chapter 3

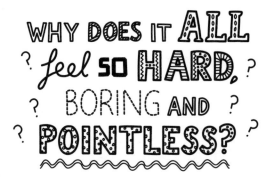

WHY DOES IT ALL feel SO HARD, BORING AND POINTLESS?

Here's what we've figured out so far. Jesus invites you into deep, real, life-transforming friendship with God—friendship that's not about *earning* anything, because Jesus has already earned it *for* you.

But, just like with any other relationship, if you want to *feel* closer to God, the best way to do that is from inside the friendship, not outside.

In other words, the more time and attention you give to Jesus, the closer to him you're likely to feel and the more of his life-transformation you're likely to experience.

Ok. But how do we actually *do* that?

Because let's be honest: the things people tell you are meant to help you grow closer to God—stuff like praying, reading the Bible, going to church—can feel pretty boring a lot of the time, right?

If Jesus wants to lead us into the best life possible, why does this stuff so often feel like such a struggle?

My friend Justin is a runner.

One of his favourite things to do on a Saturday is to get up way too early, go outside into the cold, and just *run* five kilometres. For fun.

Which is hard for me to understand—because whenever *I* go for a run, it's not fun at all. It's just painful and sweaty and exhausting.

Same activity. Two completely different experiences.

Why?

Well, partly it's because Justin and I have very different personalities. But mostly it's because Justin runs several times a week—and I run about once every seven years.

Justin has made running a regular part of his life and as a result, running has become natural and normal and even *fun* for him in a way that it just *isn't* for me.

Not only that, but he's unlocked all kinds of benefits I'm missing out on: better fitness, better sleep, stronger bones, better ability to fight disease...

I wish I had all that. I wish I could run like Justin.

And the truth is, there's nothing stopping me.

If I got up a few mornings a week and went for a run—if I just stuck with it—before long, I'd push through the sweaty, painful part to the part where it actually gets good.

The problem is, because I'm so out of practice, when my alarm goes off in the morning, it's so much easier to just roll over in bed.

And the same thing is true for the habits that help us feel closer to God: if we're out of practice, they can feel awkward and unnatural (and, honestly, kind of pointless) at first—which means it's all too easy to quit before we get to the good stuff.

And unfortunately, getting started is only part of our struggle.

My friend Chris Coffee is an incredible guitar player. Every time I see Chris play the guitar, it makes *me* want to learn to play.

And the great news is, Chris has offered several times to teach me. I even went out and bought a really nice guitar a few years ago.

So why is that guitar sitting under my bed, collecting dust?

Well, if you asked me why I haven't learned to play the guitar yet, my answer would probably be, "I just haven't had the time."

Which *feels* true.

But actually, I don't think it is.

See, I made an embarrassing discovery recently. Turns out my Nintendo Switch has a feature that tracks how many hours I've spent playing each game I own—and let's just say that even if I'd just spent *some* of those hours picking up a guitar instead of a controller, I'd probably be a pretty good musician by now.

Same deal with the hours I've spent scrolling on my phone, or watching TV, or caught up in other activities I've committed to.

It's not that any of those other things are *bad*, exactly.

But as much as I might like to tell myself I "don't have time" to learn guitar, one look at the Screen Time app on my phone tells me that's just not true.

I do have time.

I'm just spending it on other things.

And this is the same struggle we face when it comes to investing in our friendships with God: even if we like the *idea* of making time to pray or read the Bible or whatever, it's so easy to feel like we just can't fit it into our schedule.

But the truth is, we all make time for what we most value.

And so the real question isn't, "Are you busy?"—because we're all filling our time with *something*.

The real question is, "What are you busy *with*?"

But, ok, let's say you convince yourself this stuff is worth doing—and let's say you even find time in your day to make it a priority.

Even then, we have another challenge: distraction.

I sit down. I open my Bible. I start reading.

My phone buzzes next to me. I check it, read the message, send a quick reply. Then, without even really meaning to, I swipe over to Instagram. Someone's tagged me in a video. I watch it, leave a comment, scroll for a bit.

A few minutes later, I remember what I'm meant to be doing. I put down my phone and look down at my Bible again. But now my mind is starting to wander. I realise I've read a whole paragraph without even knowing what it said.

I try reading it again, but now I'm thinking about something I need to tell someone when I get to school—which gets me thinking about what I want to order for lunch today—and before I know it, it's time to get up and get out the door.

When it comes to slowing down enough to be quiet and still and focus on God, the challenge isn't just that our *lives* are busy. It's that our *minds* are busy.

There are always a thousand other things competing for our attention.

Here's my point: if feeling close to God doesn't come easily to you, it's important to realise that's *completely normal*.

We're almost all busy, distracted, and out of practice—and the problem behind all the other problems is that, like I said in the last chapter, we live in a good world that's gone wrong.

One day, Jesus will return to smash those obstacles to pieces once and for all—but in the meantime, don't be surprised if it feels like a struggle. That's not a sign you're doing something wrong.

But one of the most important things we can do as apprentices of Jesus is to keep pushing back against that lying voice telling us that it's all too hard, that it's not worth it, or that God doesn't really love us—because the more we practise living our lives the way Jesus lived *his* life, the more natural and life-changing it will become for us.

As you keep living as Jesus' apprentice, as you keep putting your trust in him, you can know for sure that he's leading and guiding and transforming you, moment by moment, day by day, bit by bit, into the person God made you to be.

And despite how hard, boring, and pointless it might feel *now*, if you stick with it, I promise it's worth it.

Ok. So how do we get started?

Chapter 4

HOW DO I GET STARTED?

There's this amazing true story in the first book of the Bible where God appears to a man named Jacob in a dream.

In his dream, Jacob sees a stairway stretching from Earth to heaven, with angels travelling up and down on it—and then God speaks to Jacob in a voice he can *actually hear*.

God promises to bless and watch over Jacob wherever he goes. He says he's going to bless the *whole world* through Jacob's family.

And then Jacob wakes up.

He understands right away that this is no ordinary dream. His sleeping brain hasn't made this vision up. The God of the universe has just spoken to him directly.

Now, my point here is not that you should expect God to start regularly showing up in your dreams. (Although

I also wouldn't put it past him; God can talk to you however he wants.)

What I most want to show you is Jacob's reaction:

> *When Jacob awoke from his sleep, he thought, "Surely the LORD is in this place, and I was not aware of it."*
> *(Genesis 28 v 16)*

Notice, Jacob didn't wake up and think, *Wow! God showed up for a minute there—but now he's gone again.*

Instead, he realised the truth: that God had been right there with Jacob *all along*; Jacob just hadn't been aware of it.

And I think there's an important lesson here for us— especially for those of us who are already living as apprentices of Jesus. One of the Bible's most mind-blowing promises is that, when you put your trust in Jesus, God's Holy Spirit comes to make his home within you (Acts 2 v 38-39).

God's Spirit is God himself, living with every follower of Jesus, helping us to know and love God, and to live his way. Which means that what was true for Jacob way back then is just as true at every moment of every day for every single apprentice of Jesus, no matter where we are:

The Lord is in this place.

We don't have to do anything to get God to show up. He's already here. The question is, "Are we aware of it?"

So how do we become aware of it?

Well, like I've already said, I think two of our major struggles here are busyness and distraction. If we want to feel closer to God, we need to learn to slow down long enough to pay attention to him.

How? Well, check out these words from Mark's biography of Jesus:

Very early in the morning, while it was still dark, Jesus got up, left the house and went off to a solitary place, where he prayed. (Mark 1 v 35)

Later, when Jesus' friends were so busy and surrounded by crowds that they didn't even have a chance to eat, Jesus told them:

"Come with me by yourselves to a quiet place and get some rest." (Mark 6 v 31)

And then in Luke's biography of Jesus, we read:

But Jesus often withdrew to lonely places and prayed.
(Luke 5 v 16)

A solitary place. A quiet place. Lonely places. These are three different descriptions of the same idea: over and over again, all through his life on Earth, Jesus deliberately made time to escape from the noise and busyness of life, to be quiet and still, and to spend time with God his Father.

If we want to feel closer to God, *this* is where we need to start. We need to make time in our day to stop everything we're doing, put away all our distractions, and just be still.

Which sounds simple enough.

But here's a little experiment for you:

Put this book down right now. Get everything out of your hands. Close your eyes. And see how long you can just be still and quiet before it drives you crazy.

How did you go?

If you're anything like me, I'm guessing it wasn't long before your mind wandered or you went reaching for something to break the boredom.

Real, deliberate stillness and quiet are so *unnatural* to us. But if we want to feel closer to God, this is where it all starts.

We fight busyness by learning to deliberately slow down.

We fight distraction by learning to deliberately focus on God.

We grow closer to God by deliberately creating space in our busy lives (and busy minds) to practise some regular habits, copied from the life of Jesus—habits designed to help us pay attention to him, to help us realise that "the LORD is in this place, and I was not aware of it".

Obviously, this is going to take practice. And, like with any new habit, it's important to start where you are, not where you think you *should* be.

Maybe one day, I'll be able to get up in the morning and run five kilometres or pick up a guitar and play whatever I want—but if I try to *start* there, I'm just going to get frustrated and disappointed.

If I want to make real progress, my best bet is to start with a simple, regular routine, and build on from there. And the same is true when it comes to the habits and practices that are going to help you feel more closely connected to God.

I love the writer Pete Greig's version of this advice:

"Keep it simple. Keep it real. Keep it up!"

We're going to spend the rest of the book figuring out how to do this—but if you want a place to start, here's my suggestion.

Get a notebook and a pen and find ten minutes at the start of your day. (I do this in the morning when I first get up, sitting in a quiet chair by the window, while I eat my breakfast.)

First, just sit there for a minute. Let yourself slow down. Be as calm and still as you can. It'll probably feel super weird at first—but just go with it.

Second, pray a short, simple prayer, inviting God into your day. Maybe something like this:

Dear God,

Thank you for this new day.

Thank you that you made me, and that you love me.

Thank you that you are always with me.

Please help me to be aware of you today.

In Jesus' name,

Amen.

Third, open your notebook and write down a few things you're grateful for. The more specific, the better. Here are a few examples from my notebook this week:

- Thanks for the school holidays.

- Thanks for pizza and board games with my friends.

- Thanks that I could hang out with my niece and nephews yesterday.

Then just read back over what you've written, taking a moment to thank God for each thing on the list. This kind of gratitude is a great way to focus your mind on the ways God has *already* been showing up in your life to love and care for you.

Stillness. Prayer. Gratitude.

Simple, right?

But if you keep going with it—if you repeat this same daily routine for a week, a month, a year—sooner or later, you'll look back and be amazed at the difference it's made.

Chapter 5

HOW (and why) SHOULD I PRAY?

When people talk about God seeming distant, one thing they often bring up is prayer.

You talk to God, but it feels pretty much like talking to yourself. You ask him for something, and he doesn't give it to you. You pray that something *won't* happen, but it happens anyway.

So why even bother praying if it doesn't really seem to *do* anything?

Well, I guess that depends what you think prayer is for.

Don't get me wrong, God *loves* to answer our prayers—and one way or another, he always does! But I think the first step towards really *enjoying* prayer is realising that it's about so much more than just getting God to do what we want.

To show you what I mean, check out the prayer that Jesus taught his first apprentices:

Our Father in heaven, hallowed be your name, your kingdom come, your will be done, on earth as it is in heaven. Give us today our daily bread. And forgive us our debts, as we also have forgiven our debtors. And lead us not into temptation but deliver us from the evil one. (Matthew 6 v 9b-13)

First, a question: Who is this prayer *to*? Who's it directed at?

I mean, God, obviously.

But the prayer doesn't start with *Dear God...*

It starts with "Our Father"—and this is a huge deal.

The word "God" means all kinds of things to all kinds of people, but here Jesus invites us to approach God with the security and closeness of a child talking to their dad.

Then again, there are plenty of different kinds of fathers, and they're not all great. So if God is our Father in heaven, what kind of father is he?

To answer that, we only need to open the Bible and look at Jesus—because Jesus says anyone who's seen him *has* seen the Father (John 14 v 9).

When you see Jesus welcoming the people everyone else is leaving out, *that's* what our Father in heaven is like.

When you see Jesus patiently sticking with his disciples—no matter how often they mess up and need to come back to him for yet another chance—*that's* what our Father in heaven is like.

When you see Jesus hanging on a cross, laying down his life to pay for all the ways we've made a mess of ours, crying out for forgiveness for the people torturing him to death, *that's* what our Father in heaven is like.

And the more we realise all this, the more it'll transform our experience of prayer.

For one thing, recognising God as your loving Father means you don't need to stress about getting the words right.

Prayer isn't a speech. It's a conversation with someone who loves you, who understands you even better than you understand yourself, and who knows what you mean, and what you need, even when you can't find the words (Romans 8 v 26). So just say whatever's on your mind and know that God gets it, and that he cares for you.

And since God is your loving Father, there's nothing you're "not allowed" to say to him.

Check out this prayer from King David:

> *My God, my God, why have you abandoned me? Why are you so far away when I groan for help? Every day I call to you, my God, but you do not answer. Every night I lift my voice, but I find no relief. (Psalm 22 v 1-2, NLT)*

Not exactly holding back, is he? He's pouring his whole heart out to God, saying *exactly* how he feels—which is how God invites *us* to come to him too.

God already knows everything you're thinking and feeling; you might as well be honest with him! And the more you learn to take all your deepest thoughts and feelings and talk them through *with* God, the more you'll discover you can trust God to help you through whatever life throws at you.

Back to Jesus' prayer.

The next thing we read is "hallowed be your name".

The basic idea here is about recognising God's greatness and love and treating him the way he deserves. Jesus wants us to pray that we would learn to love God more and more—and that the people around us who don't know him yet would come to love and honour him too.

Which brings us to "your kingdom come, your will be done, on earth as it is in heaven".

Jesus invites his apprentices to look forward with excitement to the day when he'll bring his kingdom to Earth—when he'll return to make this world our perfect home again.

In the meantime, we can ask for God's help to live as people who *already* belong to that future kingdom, here and now, today—people who are transformed by God's love so that we love him and love others.

The next part of the prayer is about asking God for what we need—but here's what I want you to notice: Jesus doesn't tell us to pray, "Give *me* today *my* daily bread."

He says, "Give *us* today *our* daily bread."

We see this same language all through the prayer: "*Our* Father ... forgive *us* ... lead *us* ... deliver *us*."

Apparently, prayer isn't just about *me*. It's about *us*.

So, the first level here is about asking God to give you *your* "daily bread". And this isn't just about food: ask him for whatever you need and thank him when he gives it to you.

The next level is praying for others—asking God to help the people around you.

But I think there's another, even deeper level to all this. Remember, God created us to join him in ruling and caring for his world, so it shouldn't surprise us that one major way God chooses to help people is through *other people*.

Which means *your* prayers are also an opportunity to tune yourself in to the ways that God might be inviting you to become his answer to *someone else's* prayers.

So ask yourself, who around you *doesn't* have their "daily

bread"? Who *doesn't* have everything they need? And how might God be inviting you to help?

How can you use what God has blessed *you* with to be a blessing to others?

Prayer is also our opportunity to ask God to "forgive us our debts" and "lead us not into temptation"—to admit when we've done wrong to him or to other people, to ask for his forgiveness, and to ask him to keep us away from whatever's going to tempt us into making those same destructive choices again.

But again, it's not just "forgive *me*"; it's "forgive *us* … as we also have forgiven our debtors".

If you're putting your trust in Jesus, God offers you unlimited forgiveness, again and again, no matter how many times you need it, because Jesus has already paid for *all* of it on the cross. But God forgiving us is meant to go hand-in-hand with us forgiving other people. Receiving God's forgiveness means learning, with the help of God's Spirit, to offer the people around us the same unlimited forgiveness Jesus offers us.

So how do we take all that and bring it into our day-to-day lives?

Well, here's what it looks like for me.

First, like I said before, I try to start each day with a few quiet moments of prayer. Before anything else—before I check my phone or worry about whatever I need to *do* that day—I take a moment to be quiet and still, to remind myself that God is right there with me, patiently waiting for me to bring my attention back to him.

I thank God for the new day.

I pray for my friends and family, and whoever else God brings to my mind.

I ask God to help me and guide me through whatever's coming up that day.

And I ask him to keep reminding me of his presence with me throughout the day—to help me notice all the ways he's blessing and caring for me, and all the opportunities he's giving me to share his love with the people around me.

Which brings me to the second way I try to make prayer a regular part of my life.

There's a part of the Bible that always used to confuse me:

> *Rejoice always, pray continually, give thanks in all circumstances; for this is God's will for you in Christ Jesus. (1 Thessalonians 5 v 16-18)*

Because what does it mean to *pray continually*? Surely God

can't want us to pray *all* the time. What about all the other stuff we need to get done?

But then I began to realise that God isn't inviting us to pray *instead* of living the rest of our lives. He's inviting us to pray *as* we live the rest of our lives.

Brother Lawrence, an apprentice of Jesus who lived 400 years ago, called this "practising the presence of God"— getting more and more into the habit of reminding ourselves of God's presence and his love. It's as simple as this: as you move through your day, as often as you think of it, just remind yourself that God is with you.

As you receive something, thank God for it.

As you realise you've messed up, tell God you're sorry.

As you chat to someone, pray for them.

It doesn't have to be some long, complicated prayer—just a simple *thank you* or *sorry* or *please help* in the back of your mind. Just a second or two.

But I've discovered that the more I practise the presence of God, the closer to him I feel, and the more of his love and joy and peace I experience.

My third daily prayer habit comes at the end of the day, as I'm lying in bed. I think back over my day and ask myself a few questions.

First, what went well? What do I have to be grateful for? I take a moment to thank God for those things.

Second, what *didn't* go well? What do I have to say sorry for, and to turn away from? I take a moment to admit those things to God, and to say sorry, knowing that he's ready and waiting to forgive me.

And third, how am I feeling at the end of the day? I try to be as honest as I can, and to pray through those feelings with God.

Don't worry about following these steps exactly. Don't even worry if you find yourself falling asleep halfway through!

The point is just to begin and end your day with God, and to process it all *with* God, the same way you would if you were talking it all out with a friend.

One last suggestion: remember that gratitude notebook I talked about in the last chapter? Consider expanding that into a prayer journal.

At the start of the day (or whenever works best), besides writing down what you're grateful for, write down what you want to ask God for, or say sorry to God for, or anything else you're feeling.

Partly, this will help to focus your attention on whatever you're praying about.

But also, like I said before, even though prayer is about *so much more* than just getting God to do what you want, God still *loves* to answer our prayers—and writing some of those prayers down gives you a great way to look back, a month or even a year from now, and realise just how many times God really *did* answer them, even if it wasn't exactly the way you expected.

Chapter 6

HOW (and why) SHOULD I READ THE BIBLE?

A few years ago, I took a bus from Jerusalem in Israel to a lookout with an amazing, panoramic view of the Judean wilderness—dry, brown hills rolling out in every direction, all scattered with rocks and dotted with scraggly little bushes. In the setting sun, it all looked kind of beautiful (in a lifeless-desert sort of way). Still, I found myself feeling extremely grateful to be there in the cool of the evening instead of the heat of the day.

Here's the thing that really blew me away, though: if I'd been standing at that same lookout around 2,000 years ago, there's a pretty good chance I would've spotted Jesus out there somewhere, doing battle with an ancient enemy of God.

This enemy, often called the devil or Satan, came to Jesus in the wilderness and tried to knock him off-course from God's plan to come to our rescue (Matthew 4 v 1-11).

The enemy didn't use physical violence; he knew he was no match for God's power. Instead, he used the same strategy he's been using since the beginning: spinning lies and deceptions designed to put God's goodness in doubt.

And how did Jesus fight back against the Enemy's lies?

The same way we need to do it: with the truth.

When the enemy suggested that Jesus couldn't trust his heavenly Father to look after him—that he should just use his power to turn some stones into bread instead—Jesus shot back with a quote from the Hebrew Bible: "People do not live by bread alone, but by every word that comes from the mouth of God" (Deuteronomy 8 v 3, NLT).

When the enemy challenged Jesus to *prove* God's love and care for him, Jesus had God's words on the tip of his tongue: "You must not test the LORD your God" (Deuteronomy 6 v 16, NLT).

When the enemy said he'd give Jesus unlimited power, if only Jesus would bow down to him, Jesus knew exactly how to respond: "You must worship the LORD your God, and serve only him" (Deuteronomy 6 v 13, NLT).

Jesus pushed back against the lies of the enemy with the truth of God's word—until eventually, the enemy gave up and left him alone.

You see this pattern all through Jesus' life: he was so familiar with the words of Scripture that, no matter what situation he found himself in, he always had the perfect wisdom of God to guide what he said and did. He knew the truth of God's faithfulness and love so deeply that he could face any situation life threw at him.

How was he so good at this?

Well, obviously it was easy for him, you might think. *Jesus was God, here on Earth.*

But remember, Jesus was also fully human, which means he didn't just get the Scriptures downloaded into his brain at birth. He got to know the Bible the same way anyone else does: by reading and listening to it, over and over again.

Which means that this kind of ready-for-anything wisdom and confidence isn't some magic superpower that Jesus is keeping all to himself.

It's something *you* can access exactly the same way he did.

God is completely unlimited in the way he speaks to people. In fact, one way or another, God never *stops* talking to us. He's constantly showing us his power and glory and kindness through the universe he's created (Psalm 19 v 1-4; Romans 1 v 20; Acts 14 v 17).

All through history, God has also spoken to his people through prophecy—messages given by his Spirit to one person, to teach and encourage others (Hebrews 1 v 1; 1 Corinthians 14 v 31). He's also appeared to people in their dreams, and in visions (Joel 2 v 28). One time, he even communicated through a talking donkey (Numbers 22 v 21-41).

But however *else* God chooses to speak to us, he'll never say anything that contradicts what he's already said in the Bible.

The Bible is where we find God's unchanging truth for everyone, everywhere, in every generation—and it's where we meet Jesus, who gives us our clearest, most easy-to-understand picture of who God is (Hebrews 1 v 2-3). Anytime we think God might be speaking to us in some *other* way, we need to compare that message to what's in the Bible and make sure it matches up.

As apprentices of Jesus, getting to know the Bible inside and out is one of the most important, most valuable ways we can grow closer to God. But the point isn't just to fill our heads with a bunch of interesting facts *about* God. It's also to hear *from* God, to grow in the wisdom we need to follow him in our everyday lives (2 Timothy 3 v 16-17).

See, the Bible isn't just a collection of great, useful wisdom for living; it's not just a record of all the times God spoke to *those people back then*.

The Bible is God's word to *you*—right here, right now, today—and you can trust him to speak to you through it every time you pick it up and read it.

But maybe you've tried this already.

Maybe you've tried reading the Bible for yourself, or sat there while other people tried to explain it to you, and you've just come away feeling either bored or confused or both.

If that's you, I totally get it. The Bible is a challenging book. But if you hang in there with it, I promise you it's absolutely worth the struggle. And for most of us, I think the first thing we need to do when it comes to the Bible is to adjust our expectations.

What I mean is that if you pick up the Bible, read a page or two, and come away feeling like you didn't fully understand it, that's completely normal—because the Bible isn't the kind of book you're meant to just pick up, read once, and go, "Great! I get it now!"

The Bible contains *deep* wisdom from God, which he wants to reveal to you over a *lifetime* of reading. There is always more to discover, more to learn, more to figure out.

Which might seem kind of overwhelming—until you remember that your main aim here is not to become an expert on a *book*; it's to get to know a *person*. It's to grow in your friendship with Jesus.

And how do you get to know a friend?

A day at a time.

When you first begin a friendship with someone, you

don't know much about them at all—but hopefully your reaction isn't, "Ugh! What a hassle! Why even bother?"

One of the *best parts* of friendship is getting to know someone better and better as you spend time with them. And the same goes for our friendship with God.

None of us will understand God completely clearly until Jesus returns and we see him face to face (1 Corinthians 13 v 12)—but in the meantime, as you follow Jesus, and as you keep coming back to the Bible, you can trust that God's Spirit will be at work in your heart and mind, helping you to get to know him better and better (John 14 v 26; 1 Corinthians 2 v 9-16).

Again, it helps to have a regular routine, so if you're looking for somewhere to start, here's what I'd suggest.

Rather than just flipping your Bible open at random, pick out *one* book and read it all the way through, a little bit each day. (If you're brand new to the Bible, I'd suggest the Gospel of Mark, which is a biography of Jesus written by a friend of Jesus' first disciples.)

Each day, before you start reading, take a moment to pray. Remind yourself that God is right there with you as you read, and ask him to show you what he wants you to understand about himself.

Then just open your Bible and read for a bit (or if reading

is a challenge for you, you might like to try *listening* to the Bible; there are plenty of great audio versions out there.)

Don't rush through. Take it slow. Read over the same bit a couple of times.

When something stands out to you, write it down in your prayer journal. Then take some time to think and pray about that idea: What is it about this part of the Bible that stood out to you? What do you think God is saying? How might he be inviting you to respond to what he's showing you? What questions do you have?

For example, here's a verse that jumped out at me as I was reading Matthew's Gospel this morning:

> *Jesus went through all the towns and villages, teaching in their synagogues, proclaiming the good news of the kingdom and healing every disease and sickness.*
> *(Matthew 9 v 35)*

I've read this part of the Bible a bunch of times, but what really stood out to me this time around was one really simple idea: Jesus didn't just sit back and wait for the people to come to him; he went to *them*—"through all the towns and villages"—searching people out, teaching and healing and sharing the good news of God's kingdom.

As I wrote that verse down in my journal, I was reminded again that *this* is what God's love is like. He's not hiding out somewhere, waiting for us to find him. In Jesus, God has come to us. He's *become* one of us, to save and rescue us—to save and rescue *me*.

I took a moment to thank God for this reminder of his love for me. I asked for his help to keep remembering that love throughout the day, and to make the most of the opportunities he would give me to share that love with the people around me.

As usual, the whole thing looked completely unimpressive on the outside. No bright lights or booming voices from heaven. But right there, in my chair by the window, while I ate my breakfast, the God of the universe welcomed me another step deeper into my friendship with him.

One last step I'd suggest as you dig into the Bible is to talk about what you've been reading and learning with other followers of Jesus. This will do a whole bunch of really valuable things:

If God has shown you something in the Bible that's helped or encouraged you, chances are it'll help and encourage the people you share it with too.

If you've got questions about what you've read, they'll be able to help you search for some answers.

And if it turns out you've misunderstood something you've read, other followers of Jesus will be able to help you get back on track.

Remember: growing closer to God is something we were always meant to do *together*.

Which brings us to our next important habit: if you want to feel closer to God, the best way to do that is in community with other followers of Jesus.

Chapter 7

HOW (and why) SHOULD I DO ALL THIS WITH OTHER PEOPLE?

So far, most of the ways of connecting with God we've been exploring have been things you can do by yourself—but that's only part of the picture. The truth is, we were never meant to follow Jesus on our own.

Way back in the very beginning, God created human beings to work *together* to rule and care for the universe he'd created (Genesis 1 v 26-28; 2 v 18-24)—and at the very *end* of the Bible, we learn that, when Jesus returns, the new creation will be filled with a crowd too big to count "from every nation, tribe, people and language", all loving and worshipping and enjoying God together, for all eternity (Revelation 7 v 9-10).

From beginning to end, growing closer to God is something we're meant to do *together*.

We see this in Jesus' own life on Earth, where he brought together a group of extremely diverse men and women—

people so different that they would *never* have hung out together, except that they were Jesus' followers (Mark 3 v 13-19; Luke 8 v 1-3).

And having lived *his* whole life together with God's people, Jesus wants *us* to do the same.

Why is this such a big deal?

Here's how one early apprentice of Jesus put it:

> *Let us hold unswervingly to the hope we profess, for he who promised is faithful. And let us consider how we may spur one another on toward love and good deeds, not giving up meeting together, as some are in the habit of doing, but encouraging one another—and all the more as you see the Day approaching.*
> *(Hebrews 10 v 23-25)*

Following Jesus is *hard* sometimes. The way he calls us to live is so different to how most other people are living, and there are times when it feels like it would be way easier to just forget the whole thing.

In moments like these, we need to encourage one another to *keep holding on* to the hope we have in Jesus, to keep living as his apprentices, to keep learning to love like he does.

We need to keep reminding each other that "the Day" is coming—the day when Jesus will return to reunite heaven and Earth and welcome his people home into never-ending life with him.

When you start to wonder whether it's all worth it, you need friends to remind you that it *absolutely* is. And in the times when *they* start to wonder whether it's all worth it, they're going to need your help too.

But there's more.

Remember how I said Jesus' first disciples were all really different to each other?

That wasn't an accident.

Think of it this way: your body has many different parts, but they're all designed to work together. A body that was all feet, or all eyes, or all tongues, would be completely useless (and kind of gross)—but when all the different parts of your body are doing what they do best, the whole thing thrives.

And according to the Bible, the church (the community of Jesus' apprentices that stretches all around the world) is kind of like that (1 Corinthians 12 v 12-27).

This pattern started with Jesus' first followers—but it didn't stop there. Two thousand years later, Jesus is still deliberately bringing together all kinds of very different people to love and look after each other, and to help each other grow.

So, for example, I have this one friend at church who is incredible at playing the piano; her music is such a gift to our church family.

Another one of my church friends is particularly enthusiastic about praying for other people. I don't know how to explain it exactly, but there's something about the way she prays that just fills you up inside. God seems to have this special way of using her prayers to remind you that, whatever's going on, he's got it under control and you're going to be ok.

I have another friend who's excellent at baking. Every now and then, he'll drop by with a batch of phenomenal chocolate chip cookies, just to encourage me or thank me for something.

Then there's my friend who is really good at finding the lonely person who needs someone to talk to. God has given her this amazing gift of noticing the person no one else is noticing, and welcoming them into the group.

I also have this other friend who is really great at talking honestly about her own struggles in a way that makes people feel less alone in *their* struggles. Life is not easy for her, but as she keeps following Jesus, I can see how God is working in her to transform not just *her* life, but other people's lives as well.

These friends are all such amazing, generous gifts from God—and when we meet together as God's people, we bring all of those gifts together and everyone benefits.

We bless and encourage each other. We fill each other up. We grow closer to one another, and we grow closer to God as well.

And, by the way, none of these people I've just mentioned are the *adults* at my church. They're all teenagers in the youth group I help lead each week. I mean, sure, the adults have plenty to contribute too; but my point is, whoever you are—however young or old you are, or however new you are to following Jesus—God has created you with your own unique gifts to share with his people. (And if you're not sure what yours are yet, meeting regularly with God's people is a *great* way to start figuring it out!)

If you want to feel closer to God, you *need* to stay connected to his people.

The most obvious way to do this is by joining a church, but depending on your age and your situation, you could also consider joining a church youth group, or a mid-week Bible study group, or the Christian group at your school if you have one—or all of the above!

However you choose to do it, the point is not to attend as many *events* as you can (as helpful as those can be.) It's to find a community of *people* who will help you grow closer to Jesus.

If you happen to have tons in common with those people, great! But even if you don't—even if you're the only one your age or if no one else there is into the same stuff you are—stick with it, because what you *do* have in common is Jesus, and that's way more important than anything else.

But whatever gathering with other apprentices of Jesus looks like in your situation, here's my number one tip for getting the most out of it:

Go all in.

Don't just sit back and *watch* what's going on. Join in with everything, as much as you can. Sing along with the songs. Pray along with the prayers. When someone gets up to read the Bible, open your Bible and read along. Because the more you join in, the more you'll get out of it.

Are you still not sure you even believe this stuff yet? Pray anyway! What's the worst that could happen?

Are you a terrible singer? Me too! Sing big and loud anyway. Trust me: no one will care. Besides, you're not auditioning for a choir—you're singing to *God*, and he thinks you sound great!

(Side note: I wish I had space in this book for a whole chapter on the incredible power of music to help us feel closer to God—but the short version is that music has this unique way of driving the truth about God deeper into our hearts and minds. There's nothing like singing God's praises *with* other people, but don't stop there! Find yourself a playlist of great music full of the truth about God, and make it part of your day-to-day listening.)

You might go to a church with thousands of people, a stage full of professional musicians, and world-class Bible teaching—or you might go to a church with four old ladies, a creaky pipe organ, and an honestly-kind-of-boring minister who's just up there doing their best.

But Jesus has promised that, whenever and wherever his people gather in his name, he'll be right there with them, and his Spirit will be working to grow and transform them (Matthew 18 v 20; 28 v 20; John 14 v 26). Which means that, whatever gathering of God's people you're part of, Jesus is part of it too, and you can trust him to meet you there.

So find a group of God's people to follow Jesus with—and go all in.

Chapter 8

HOW MUCH TIME DO I HAVE TO SPEND ON ALL THIS?

As we've been exploring all these habits and practices that can help you feel closer to God, you may have found another question floating to the front of your mind:

How much time is all this stuff meant to take, exactly?

Obviously, it's hard to keep *any* relationship strong without investing some kind of quality time with that person—so how much time each day does Jesus want us to invest in our friendship with him?

Imagine a pie chart of your week. The bigger the slice, the more time each activity takes up. It might look something like the chart on the next page:

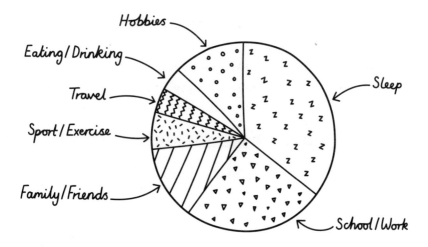

Some slices of your pie, you don't have much control over.

Before you even get started, sleep knocks out at least a third of your time (or that's how much the research tells us we *should* be getting, anyway.)

Then there's school—or, as you get older, work—which takes up another big slice.

Hopefully, your family and friends also get a decent-sized slice.

Then there's time you (hopefully) spend on some kind of sport or exercise, the time you spend eating and drinking, the time it takes to travel from place to place—

and, hopefully, after all of that, you still have some free time left over for whatever other hobbies or activities you enjoy.

If you're anything like me, you already feel a bit overwhelmed sometimes by everything you need to get done. And so where does being an apprentice of Jesus fit into all of this? If this pie chart paints a picture of your week, how big should your *Jesus* slice be?

Is Jesus ok with a little sliver of the pie—maybe something like the size of the *eating and drinking* slice? Or does he want more than that? A quarter of the pie, maybe? A third?

Actually, it's even more than that.

See, the truth is, Jesus doesn't just want a *slice* of your time.

He wants the whole pie.

Now, at first, that might sound completely ridiculous. Impossible, even. I mean, what does Jesus want us to do—quit our lives, run away to a cabin in the woods, and stay up all day and night reading the Bible?

Well, no.

It's like what I was saying about prayer before. When Jesus says he wants us to spend our whole lives following him and growing closer to him, that doesn't mean we follow Jesus *instead* of eating or sleeping or working or playing; it means we follow Jesus *while* we're doing all those things.

Yes, being an apprentice of Jesus will mean setting aside some particular time to practise the habits we've been talking about—time to sit in the quiet and focus on God, time to pray, time to read the Bible, time to meet with other followers of Jesus.

All those things are extremely valuable; they're what apprentices of Jesus have been doing for thousands of years now.

But remember, none of those things are the *point* of all this.

The point of being an apprentice of Jesus is to *become like Jesus*. It's to let his love and joy and peace transform our *whole* lives—every single moment. It's to let God's Spirit grow us up into the people we were always meant to be (Romans 12 v 1-2).

We change our habits so that, through the power of God's Holy Spirit, those habits can change us.

Jesus wants to grow us up into people who live every moment of every day with an awareness of his closeness and his love—people who are so filled up with the love of Jesus that it overflows into the lives of everyone around us.

Jesus wants to teach us to move through our days, noticing and thanking God for all the little signs of his goodness to us, and keeping an eye out for the ways he's inviting us to join in with what he's doing in the world.

I love the way pastor Jon Tyson puts it. He talks about walking to every room with the same question: *God, where have you already been working to grow your kingdom and share your love—and how can I get on board with that?*

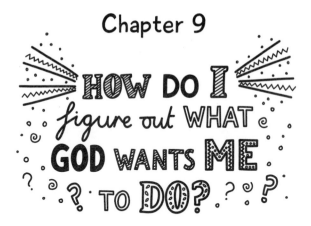

Chapter 9

HOW DO I figure out WHAT GOD WANTS ME TO DO?

So far in this book, I've tried to outline a bunch of *general* wisdom about following Jesus—habits that can help anyone, anywhere grow closer to him. But what if we want to know what to do in a *specific* situation? What if you have a big decision in front of you, and you don't know what to do? Is there any way to get God's help with *that*?

My favourite description of being an apprentice of Jesus comes from pastor John Mark Comer: "Be with Jesus. Become like Jesus. Do what he would do if he were you."

We've talked a bunch about *being with Jesus* already. We do this whenever we make time to pray, or reflect on the Bible, or just sit in the quiet and focus on Jesus. And we do it when we practise the presence of God—when we turn our focus back to Jesus throughout the day and let him remind us of his love for us.

And as we keep *being with Jesus*, we can trust that God's Spirit is right there with us, helping us to *become like Jesus*, transforming us to become more and more like the one we're following (Galatians 4 v 19; Ephesians 1 v 17-21; Philippians 1 v 4-6).

Which brings us to step three: *Do what he would do if he were you.*

In other words, if Jesus were living *your* life—if he were in your situation, with your family and friends, facing the challenges you're facing today—what would he do?

Sometimes the answer is obvious: if you're choosing between forgiving your friend for that unkind thing they said or punching them in the face, it's pretty clear that Jesus would choose the first option.

Other times, it's much harder to figure out.

But if you want to know what God wants you to do in any situation, asking, *What would Jesus do if he were me?* is a great place to start.

And for our clearest answer to *that* question, we need to keep coming back to what Jesus has shown us about himself in the Bible.

So, for example, let's say you make a new friend who's just arrived from a different city. They invite you to their birthday party, and you say you'll come. But then another friend calls: your favourite band is in town, and they have a spare ticket with your name on it. The only catch? The concert is the same night as the birthday party.

What should you do?

Well, what would Jesus do if he were you?

For starters, *whatever* Jesus did, his top priority would be to love God and love other people (Matthew 22 v 37-40). He wouldn't just do what *he* wanted to do; he'd do what was best for his friends (Philippians 2 v 3-8).

Jesus would also keep his word (Matthew 5 v 37), so one important thing to consider here is that you've *already* told your new friend you'll go to their party; saying *yes* to the concert would mean breaking that commitment.

Above all, Jesus says to "do to others what you would have them do to you" (Matthew 7 v 12)—which, in this situation, means asking, *If I were the one who'd just moved to a new city, how would I hope my new friends would treat me?*

So is there a 100% clear and obvious answer here? I don't think so. It's complicated. The Bible doesn't tell you *what* to decide in this situation, but it does give you lots of wisdom about *how* to decide.

So here's what I think I'd do:

Honestly, what I'd probably *want* to do is go to the concert—but what I'd feel like I *should* do is go to the party. But before I made my choice, I'd try to figure out how much it mattered to my new friend that I came to their party.

Are there 50 other people going? Then maybe skipping the party isn't going to make much difference after all. Maybe I can call my friend, explain the situation honestly, and organise to hang out with them some other time.

But if it turns out their party is just them and the three new people they've met since moving here... then bailing is a way bigger deal, right? So as much as I'd *love* to go to the concert, maybe what *I* want is actually not the most important thing right now. Maybe I should show up to the party after all.

Like I said, it's complicated. But the more we get to know Jesus, the more we can figure out what *he* would do in our situation, and the more that will lead us to wiser, more loving choices.

But I think there's another layer to all this.

Remember, if you've put your trust in Jesus, you have God's Holy Spirit working in your life to help you follow Jesus—and God's Spirit can speak to you whenever and wherever and however he wants.

So as you practise all the things we've been talking about in this book—as you pray, or read the Bible, or sit with God in the quiet, or talk to a friend, or listen to a sermon at church—you may get the sense that God is trying to get your attention, that there's some specific thing he's wanting you to do.

This might be a thought that pops into your head as you pray, or a verse that jumps out at you as you read the Bible, or a wise word from a friend that seems extra-important somehow. Something that makes you go, *I think God wants me to pay attention to this.*

So how do you figure out what to do with *that*?

How do you tell the difference between a sign from God and a coincidence, or between a thought God's Spirit brought into your mind and something you just came up with on your own?

I wish I had a simple, straightforward answer for you. But remember, we're getting to know a person here, not cracking a secret code. What I *can* give you are a few important pointers.

First, as we saw earlier, however else God speaks to you, he'll never go against what he's already revealed about himself in the Bible—so you can be sure that any thought or idea that doesn't match up with the Bible hasn't come from God.

Second, God will never go against his own character. God is compassionate and gracious, slow to anger, and overflowing with love and faithfulness (Exodus 34 v 6)— so you can be sure that any thought or idea that doesn't match up with that hasn't come from God either.

Third, remember that God has also given us *each other* to help us grow closer to him. So whatever you're trying to figure out, talk it through with some other followers of Jesus who you know and trust, and listen to what they have to say about it all.

And if that all still feels a bit vague or weird or confusing, pastor Timothy Keller has some great advice for us. He says that, yes, God's guidance is something God *gives*— but more often it's something God *does*.

Think of it like this. Imagine yourself steering a boat down a river with all different branching paths and streams—all kinds of different directions you might head in.

God *sometimes* acts like the navigator of your boat, standing beside you with a map, whispering directions into your ear, telling you exactly where you should go next.

But more often, God acts less like a navigator and more like *the river itself*, guiding you through your life, whether you notice him doing it or not.

So when you have a choice to make, pray about it. Talk about it with people you trust. Do your best to answer the question, *What would Jesus do if he were me?*

And then just go ahead and make the best choice you can.

If it turns out to be *exactly* the decision Jesus would have made in your place—great!

And if it turns out you got it wrong, that's ok too, because you can't ruin God's good plans with your bad decisions.

Even if you mess things up completely, God will *keep guiding you forward*, taking all your successes *and* all your failures, and working them together for good in the end (Romans 8 v 28; Genesis 50 v 20).

There have been plenty of times in my life when I've felt lost, confused about what to do, and like God was far-off and distant—times when the best I could do was make a decision and see what happened next.

There have also been times in my life when I've felt *sure* I knew what God wanted me to do next, only to discover that he had something completely different in mind.

But in the end, one thing has always been true: sooner or later, I've looked back and realised that God still knew exactly what *he* was doing, even if I had no idea what *I* was doing.

And so, sure, on one level, this stuff might feel really complicated. But on another level, it's actually really simple. Because in the end, all you really need to do is stick with Jesus, make the best choices you know how to make, and then *relax*, trusting that God is strong and kind and faithful enough to take care of the rest.

Chapter 10

There will be days when all of this feels so easy. As you follow Jesus, you'll have days when God feels so incredibly real and close and obvious—days when doubting that he exists, or that he loves you, will seem like the most ridiculous thing in the world.

And then there'll be the other days.

The days when God feels far off.

The days when the Bible feels like an old, dead book and prayer just feels like talking to the ceiling.

The days when it feels like maybe you're just imagining the whole thing.

As we've been exploring in this book, there are all kinds of habits from the life of Jesus that can help you have more and more good days than bad days.

There are also a bunch of common-sense lifestyle things you can do.

For example, how much sleep are you getting?

One thing I try really hard to do, no matter how full my life gets, is to get at least eight hours of sleep every night.

Partly, this is because getting to bed at a sensible time makes it easier to get up the next morning early enough to spend some time with Jesus before school.

But getting enough sleep also means I head into each day with more energy and focus to spend on paying attention to God and loving the people around me.

Another lifestyle habit I'd suggest is to avoid looking at your phone (or any other screen) for the first hour after you wake up in the morning—because what you focus on first thing in the morning has a huge impact on the rest of your day.

Which do you think has a better chance of filling you up with love and joy and peace for the day ahead—20 minutes with Jesus first thing in the morning, or 20 minutes with the internet?

Building choices like these into your life will help set you up for success in all the other habits we've been exploring in this book. Which, like I said, will help you have more and more good days than bad days.

Even so, there'll still be days when God feels true and real and close—and other days where you feel like giving up on the whole thing.

And on *both* those kinds of days, here's what's really important to keep in mind:

Your feelings matter; they're incredibly important. But they aren't the whole truth.

See, here's the thing: your feelings about God, and your experience of his closeness, will *absolutely* be influenced by God's Holy Spirit as he works in your life to remind you of his love, and to help you become more and more like Jesus.

But your feelings about God, and your experience of his closeness, will *also* be influenced by how much sleep you got last night, and by the kind of day you're having, and by what you ate for breakfast this morning.

Your feelings matter—but they aren't the whole truth.

Your feelings are your mind's and your body's *responses* to what's happening in your life. Sometimes those feeling match up with how things really are, and sometimes they don't.

Your feelings can change from day to day, and even from moment to moment.

That doesn't mean you should ignore them, or pretend they aren't there. We need to be honest about our feelings—to feel them all the way through.

But through it all, what's so important to remember is that our hope is not in our feelings *about* Jesus. Our hope is in Jesus himself—in God's promise that he will never abandon his children, and that he's with us wherever we go, whether that *feels* true or not (Deuteronomy 31 v 6; Matthew 28 v 20; Hebrews 13 v 5).

However close or far away God might feel on a particular day, or in a particular moment, his promise for everyone who puts their trust in Jesus is that "he who began a good work in you will carry it on to completion until the day of Christ Jesus" (Philippians 1 v 6).

In other words, Jesus has already lived the perfect life of love that you could never live.

He's already given up his life in your place to demolish every barrier standing between you and God, and to welcome you home into life forever with him.

He's already risen from the dead, proving that the power of death has been defeated once and for all.

He's already given you his Spirit to lead you and guide you into the fullness of life that he created you for.

Do you *really* think he's going to give up on you now?

So, with all of that said, what should I do on the mornings when I wake up before my alarm and jump out of bed, full of joy—the days when Jesus feels close and obvious and real—the days when I *can't wait* to open up my Bible and see what God wants to teach me today?

I should pray to the God I *know* is there, thanking him for his goodness to me, telling him how I feel, and asking for his help in every situation.

I should read the Bible with my heart and my mind wide open to discover what God might be waiting to show me.

I should talk to my Christian friends or family, and remind them that following Jesus is all absolutely worth it, even on the days when it doesn't feel worth it.

I should get out into the world and make the most of every opportunity he gives me to love him and love the people around me.

And what should I do on the days when I sleep through my alarm—the days when I'm exhausted and stressed and it all feels kind of made up?

I should pray to the God I'm only half-convinced is there, thanking him for his goodness to me, telling him how I feel, and asking for his help in every situation.

I should read the Bible with my heart and my mind wide open to discover what God might be waiting to show me—

even if it just feels dead and boring right now.

I should talk to my Christian friends or family, and let *them* remind *me* that it's all absolutely worth it, even on the days when it doesn't feel worth it.

And I should get out into the world and make the most of every opportunity he gives me to love him and love the people around me.

Because my feelings matter—but they're not the whole truth.

And what I've discovered as I've stuck with Jesus through the good days and bad days (and the good months and bad months) is that Jesus is faithful and true, even on the days when I struggle to believe it.

I am so far from being an expert on any of this stuff.

But little by little, as I practise following Jesus, I'm learning—not just as an idea, but as my own real-life experience—that the way of Jesus really is the truest, best, most life-giving way to live.

I'm learning to rest in God's promise that "neither death nor life, neither angels nor demons, neither the present nor the future, nor any powers, neither height nor depth, nor anything else in all creation, will be able to separate us from the love of God that is in Christ Jesus our Lord" (Romans 8 v 38-39).

And as I look back on the years I've spent following Jesus, I realise that I'm actually experiencing the kind of complete, caterpillar-to-butterfly transformation I talked about, way back at the beginning of this book.

Not all at once, obviously.

Not in some big, dramatic way.

But little by little, as I live each day with Jesus, I can see how he's changing me—helping me to know the truth of his love and power in my head *and* in my heart.

And as you keep trusting in Jesus, I know he'll do the same for you.

References

As ever, the reason this book exists isn't because I'm some kind of brilliant Bible expert, but because I'm standing on the shoulders of giants.

As I was starting work on the first chapter, I read a great interview with Timothy Keller in the New York Times (*How a Cancer Diagnosis Makes Jesus' Death and Resurrection Mean More*), which helped clarify my thinking on the difference between believing God's love and feeling God's love.

I mentioned this already in the book, but I want to say again how grateful I am for Dallas Willard's language around being an apprentice of Jesus.

This book owes a huge debt to John Mark Comer's teaching on practising the way of Jesus. He's the one who said the question isn't, "How much do you have to do to get God to love and accept you?", but, "How much space do you want to open up in your life to experience God's love first-hand?"

Pete Greig, co-founder of the 24-7 Prayer movement, has written two great books that were a huge help to me as I wrote this one: *How to Pray: A Simple Guide for Normal People* and *How to Hear God: A Simple Guide for Normal People.*

The "Jesus wants the whole pie" idea in Chapter 8 is something I first encountered in a sermon Jeff Manion preached at Ada Bible Church.

Other books that have helped me along in my own journey of feeling closer to God include *The Ruthless Elimination of Hurry* by John Mark Comer, *Sacred Fire* by Ronald Rolheiser, *Beautiful Resistance* by Jon Tyson, and *The Deeply Formed Life* by Rich Villodas.

Thank yous

Thanks to Rachel Jones for being such an insightful and patient editor, to André Parker and Emma Randall for your amazing design work, and to the whole team at TGBC for getting behind this series and helping it to be the best it can be.

Thanks to Micah Ford, Corlette Graham, Rosie Harris, Rowan McAuley, Charlie McQueen, and Denin Spencer, who read this book first.

Thanks to the staff, students and families of PLC Sydney. It is one of the great privileges of my life to share the good news of Jesus with you every week. Thanks in particular to my 2022 Year 5 classes for your encouragement and feedback on this book.

Thanks to Mum and Dad for the countless hours you've poured into talking through my big questions about God over the past 30+ years.

Thanks to Katie and Waz, Phil and Meredith, and Kerryn and Andrew, for your constant love, support, wisdom, and encouragement.

Thanks to Hattie, Liam, and Alec, for helping me see the love of God more clearly. May you grow up full of big questions, and may you keep turning back to our great king Jesus for the answers.

Thanks to Tom French for being a brilliant writing and podcasting buddy.

Last but not least, thanks to my church family at Abbotsford Presbyterian. In particular, a huge shout-out to the whole crew at YCentral—may this book help you to see even more clearly the abundant love God has for you in Jesus.

Keep asking big questions

△ △△△ △ △△ △ △△ △

 thegoodbook.co.uk/big-questions
thegoodbook.com/big-questions
thegoodbook.com.au/big-questions

Also by Chris Morphew

A 100-day devotional journey through Mark's fast-paced, action-packed story—bringing you face to face with Jesus: the one who changes everything.

thegoodbook.co.uk/best-news-ever
thegoodbook.com/best-news-ever
thegoodbook.com.au/best-news-ever

thegoodbook

COMPANY

BIBLICAL | RELEVANT | ACCESSIBLE

At The Good Book Company, we are dedicated to helping Christians and local churches grow. We believe that God's growth process always starts with hearing clearly what he has said to us through his timeless word—the Bible.

Ever since we opened our doors in 1991, we have been striving to produce Bible-based resources that bring glory to God. We have grown to become an international provider of user-friendly resources to the Christian community, with believers of all backgrounds and denominations using our books, Bible studies, devotionals, evangelistic resources, and DVD-based courses.

We want to equip ordinary Christians to live for Christ day by day, and churches to grow in their knowledge of God, their love for one another, and the effectiveness of their outreach.

Call us for a discussion of your needs or visit one of our local websites for more information on the resources and services we provide.

Your friends at The Good Book Company

thegoodbook.com | thegoodbook.co.uk
thegoodbook.com.au | thegoodbook.co.nz
thegoodbook.co.in